The Constitution of the
State of Hawaii:
A Quick Reference Guide

Bootblack Budget Books
Copyright 2018 ©
ISBN-13: 978-1985898271
ISBN-10: 1985898276

Contents:

Preamble – Page 21

Article I: Bill of Rights – Page 22

Section 1. Political Power

Section 2. Rights of Individuals

Section 3. Equality of Rights

Section 4. Freedom of Religion, Speech, Press, Assembly and Petition

Section 5. Due Process and Equal Protection

Section 6. Right to Privacy

Section 7. Searches, Seizures and Invasion of Privacy

Section 8. Rights of Citizens

Section 9. Enlistment; Segregation

Section 10. Indictment; Preliminary Hearing; Information; Double Jeopardy; Self-Incrimination

Section 11. Grand Jury Counsel

Section 12. Bail; Excessive Punishment

Section 13. Trial by Jury, Civil Cases

Section 14. Rights of Accused

Section 15. Habeas Corpus and Suspension of Laws

Section 16. Supremacy of Civil Power

Section 17. Right to Bear Arms

Section 18. Quartering of Soldiers

Section 19. Imprisonment for Debt

Section 20. Eminent Domain

Section 20. Limitations of Special Privilege

Section 21. Construction

Section 22. Marriage

Section 23. Public Access to Information Concerning Persons Convicted of Certain Offenses

Section 24. Sexual Assault Crimes Against Minors

Article II: Suffrage and Elections – Page 28

Section 1. Qualifications

Section 2. Disqualification

Section 3. Residence

Section 4. Registration; Voting

Section 5. Campaign Fund, Spending Limits

Section 6. Campaign Contributions Limits

Section 7. Resignation from Public Office

Section 8. General, Special and Primary Elections

Section 9. Presidential Preference Primary

Section 10. Contested Elections

Article III: The Legislature – Page 30

Section 1. Legislative Power

Section 2. Composition of Senate

Section 3. Composition of House of Representatives

Section 4. Election of Members; Term

Section 5. Vacancies

Section 6. Qualifications of Members

Section 7. Privileges of Members

Section 8. Disqualifications of Members

Section 9. Legislative Allowance

Section 10. Sessions

Section 11. Adjournment

Section 12. Organization; Discipline; Rules; Procedure

Section 13. Quorum; Compulsory Attendance

Section 14. Bills; Enactment

Section 15. Passage of Bills

Section 16. Approval or Veto; Reconsideration after Adjournment

Section 17. Procedures Upon Veto

Section 18. Punishment of Nonmembers

Section 19. Impeachment

Article IV: Reapportionment – Page 39

Section 1. Reapportionment Years

Section 2. Reapportionment Commission

Section 3. Chief Election Officer

Section 4. Apportionment Among Basic Island Units

Section 5. Minimum Representation for Basic Island Units

Section 6. Apportionment Within Basic Island Units

Section 7. Election of Senators After Reapportionment

Section 8. Staggered Terms for The Senate

Section 9. Congressional Redistricting for United States House of Representatives

Section 10. Mandamus and Judicial Review

Article V: The Executive – Page 45

Section 1. Establishment of The Executive

Section 2. Lieutenant Governor

Section 3. Compensation: Governor, Lieutenant Governor

Section 4. Succession to Governorship; Absence or Disability of Governor

Section 5. Executive Powers

Section 6. Executive and Administrative Offices and Departments

Article VI: The Judiciary – Page 49

Section 1. Judicial Power

Section 2. Supreme Court; Intermediate Appellate Court; Circuit Courts

Section 3. Appointment of Justices And Judges; Qualifications for Appointment; Tenure; Retirement

Section 4. Judicial Selection Commission

Section 5. Retirement; Removal; Discipline

Section 6. Administration

Section 7. Rules

Article VII: Taxation and Finance – Page 54

Section 1. Taxing Power Inalienable

Section 2. Income Taxation

Section 3. Tax Review Commission

Section 4. Appropriations for Private Purposes Prohibited

Section 5. Expenditure Controls

Section 6. Disposition of Excess Revenues

Section 7. Council on Revenues

Section 8. The Budget

Section 9. Legislative Appropriations; Procedures; Expenditure Ceiling; General Fund Expenditure Ceiling

Section 10. Auditor

Section 11. Lapsing of Appropriations

Section 12. Definitions; Issuance of Indebtedness

Section 13. Debt Limit; Exclusions

Article VIII: Local Government – Page 68

Section 1. Creation; Powers of Political Subdivisions

Section 2. Local Self-Government; Charter

Section 3. Taxation And Finance

Section 4. Mandates; Accrued Claims

Section 5. Transfer of Mandated Programs

Section 6. Statewide Laws

Article IX: Public Health and Welfare – Page 70

Section 1. Public Health

Section 2. Care of Handicapped Persons

Section 3. Public Assistance

Section 4. Economic Security of The Elderly

Section 5. Housing, Slum Clearance, Development and Rehabilitation

Section 6. Management of State Population Growth

Section 7. Public Sightliness and Good Order

Section 8. Preservation of a Healthful Environment

Section 9. Cultural Resources

Section 10. Public Safety

Article X: Public Education – Page 72

Section 1. Public Education

Section 2. Board of Education

Section 3. Power of The Board of Education

Section 4. Hawaiian Education Program

Section 5. University of Hawaii

Section 6. Board of Regents; Powers

Article XI: Conservation, Control and Development of Resources - Page 74

Section 1. Conservation And Development of Resources

Section 2. Management And Disposition of Natural Resources

Section 3. Agricultural Lands

Section 4. Public Land Banking

Section 5. General Laws Required; Exceptions

Section 6. Marine Resources

Section 7. Water Resources

Section 8. Nuclear Energy

Section 9. Environmental Rights

Section 10. Farm and Home Ownership

Section 11. Exclusive Economic Zone

Article XII: Hawaiian Affairs – Page 78

Section 1. Hawaiian Homes Commission Act

Section 2. Acceptance of Compact

Section 3. Compact Adoption; Procedures After Adoption

Section 4. Public Trust

Section 5. Office of Hawaiian Affairs; Establishment of Board of Trustees

Section 6. Powers of Board of Trustees

Section 7. Traditional and Customary Rights

Article XIII: Organization; Collective Bargaining – Page 82

Section 1. Private Employees

Section 2. Public Employees

Article XIV: Code of Ethics – Page 83

Section 1. Code of Ethics

**Article XV: State Boundaries; Capital;
Flag; Language and Motto** – Page 84

Section 1. Boundaries

Section 2. Capital

Section 3. State Flag

Section 4. Official Languages

Section 5. Motto

Article XVI: General and Miscellaneous Provisions – Page 85

Section 1. Civil Service

Section 2. Employees Retirement System

Section 3. Disqualifications From Public Office or Employment

Section 4. [3.5] Salary Commission

Section 5. Oath of Office

Section 6. Oath of Office

Section 7. Intergovernmental Relations

Section 8. Federal Lands

Section 9. Compliance with Trust

Section 10. Administration of Undisposed Lands

Section 11. Tax Exemption of Federal Property

Section 12. Hawaii National Park

Section 13. Judicial Rights

Section 14. Quieting Title

Section 15. Plain Language

Section 16. Titles, Subtitles; Construction

Section 17. General Power

Section 18. Provisions are Self-Executing

Article XVII: Revision and Amendment – Page 90

Section 1. Methods of Proposal

Section 2. Constitutional Convention

Section 3. Amendments Proposed by Legislature

Section 4. Veto

Section 5. Conflicting Revisions or Amendments

Article XVIII: Schedule – Page 94

Section 1. Districting and Apportionment

Section 2. 1978 Senatorial Elections

Section 3. Salaries of Legislators

Section 4. Effective Date for Term Limitations for Governor and Lieutenant Governor

Section 5. Judiciary: Transition; Effective Date

Section 6. Effective Date And Application of Real Property Tax Transfer

Section 7. 1978 Board of Education Elections

Section 8. Effective Date for Office of Hawaiian Affairs

Section 9. Continuity of Laws

Section 10. Debts

Section 11. Residence, Other Qualifications

Section 12. Board of Education Transition;

Section 13. Effective Date

Preamble

We, the people of Hawaii, grateful for Divine Guidance, and mindful of our Hawaiian heritage and uniqueness as an island State, dedicate our efforts to fulfill the philosophy decreed by the Hawaii State motto, "Ua mau ke ea o ka aina i ka pono."
We reserve the right to control our destiny, to nurture the integrity of our people and culture, and to preserve the quality of life that we desire.

We reaffirm our belief in a government of the people, by the people and for the people, and with an understanding and compassionate heart toward all the peoples of the earth, do hereby ordain and establish this constitution for the State of Hawaii.

Federal Constitution Adopted

The Constitution of the United States of America is adopted on behalf of the people of the State of Hawaii.

ARTICLE I: BILL OF RIGHTS

Section 1. Political Power

All political power of this State is inherent in the people and the responsibility for the exercise thereof rests with the people. All government is founded on this authority.

Section 2. Rights of Individuals

All persons are free by nature and are equal in their inherent and inalienable rights. Among these rights are the enjoyment of life, liberty and the pursuit of happiness, and the acquiring and possessing of property. These rights cannot endure unless the people recognize their corresponding obligations and responsibilities.

Section 3. Equality of Rights

Equality of rights under the law shall not be denied or abridged by the State on account of sex. The legislature shall have the power to enforce, by appropriate legislation, the provisions of this section.

Section 4. Freedom of Religion, Speech, Press, Assembly and Petition

No law shall be enacted respecting an establishment of religion, or prohibiting the free exercise thereof, or abridging the freedom of speech or of the press or the right of the people peaceably to assemble and to petition the government for a redress of grievances.

Section 5. Due Process and Equal Protection

No person shall be deprived of life, liberty or property without due process of law, nor be denied the equal protection of the laws, nor be denied the enjoyment of the person's civil rights or be discriminated against in the exercise thereof because of race, religion, sex or ancestry.

Section 6. Right to Privacy

The right of the people to privacy is recognized and shall not be infringed without the showing of a compelling state interest. The legislature shall take affirmative steps to implement this right.

Section 7. Searches, Seizures and Invasion of Privacy

The right of the people to be secure in their persons, houses, papers and effects against unreasonable searches, seizures and invasions of privacy shall not be violated; and no warrants shall issue but upon probable cause, supported by oath or affirmation, and particularly describing the place to be searched and the persons or things to be seized or the communications sought to be intercepted.

Section 8. Rights of Citizens

No citizen shall be disfranchised, or deprived of any of the rights or privileges secured to other citizens, unless by the law of the land.

Section 9. Enlistment; Segregation

No citizen shall be denied enlistment in any military organization of this State nor be segregated therein because of race, religious principles or ancestry.

Section 10. Indictment; Preliminary Hearing; Information; Double Jeopardy; Self-Incrimination

No person shall be held to answer for a capital or otherwise infamous crime, unless on a presentment or indictment of a grand jury or upon a finding of probable cause after a preliminary hearing held as provided by law or upon information in writing signed by a legal prosecuting officer under conditions and in accordance with procedures that the legislature may provide, except in cases arising in the armed forces when in actual service in time of war or public danger; nor shall any person be subject for the same offense to be twice put in jeopardy; nor shall any person be compelled in any criminal case to be a witness against oneself.

Section 11. Grand Jury Counsel

Whenever a grand jury is impaneled, there shall be an independent counsel appointed as provided by law to advise the members of the grand jury regarding matters brought before it. Independent counsel shall be selected from among those persons licensed to practice law by the supreme court of the State and shall not be a public employee. The term and compensation for independent counsel shall be as provided by law.

Section 12. Bail; Excessive Punishment

Excessive bail shall not be required, nor excessive fines imposed, nor cruel or unusual punishment inflicted. The court may dispense with bail if reasonably satisfied that the defendant or witness will appear when directed, except for a defendant charged with an offense punishable by life imprisonment.

Section 13. Trial by Jury, Civil Cases

In suits at common law where the value in controversy shall exceed five thousand dollars, the right of trial by jury shall be preserved. The legislature may provide for a verdict by not less than three-fourths of the members of the jury.

Section 14. Rights of Accused

In all criminal prosecutions, the accused shall enjoy the right to a speedy and public trial by an impartial jury of the district wherein the crime shall have been committed, which district shall have been previously ascertained by law, or of such other district to which the prosecution may be removed with the consent of the accused; to be informed of the nature and cause of the accusation; to be confronted with the witnesses against the accused, provided that the legislature may provide by law for the inadmissibility of privileged confidential communications between an alleged crime victim and the alleged crime victim's physician, psychologist, counselor or licensed mental health professional; to have compulsory process for obtaining witnesses in the accused's favor; and to have the assistance of counsel for the accused's defense. Juries, where the crime charged is serious, shall consist of twelve persons. The State shall provide counsel for an indigent defendant charged with an offense punishable by imprisonment.

Section 15. Habeas Corpus and Suspension of Laws

The privilege of the writ of habeas corpus shall not be suspended unless, when in cases of rebellion or invasion, the public safety may require it.

The power of suspending the privilege of the writ of habeas corpus, and the laws or the execution thereof, shall never be exercised except by the legislature, or by authority derived from it to be exercised in such particular cases only as the legislature shall expressly prescribe.

Section 16. Supremacy of Civil Power

The military shall be held in strict subordination to the civil power.

Section 17. Right to Bear Arms

A well regulated militia being necessary to the security of a free state, the right of the people to keep and bear arms shall not be infringed.

Section 18. Quartering of Soldiers

No soldier or member of the militia shall, in time of peace, be quartered in any house, without the consent of the owner or occupant, nor in time of war, except in a manner provided by law.

Section 19. Imprisonment for Debt

There shall be no imprisonment for debt.

Section 20. Eminent Domain

Private property shall not be taken or damaged for public use without just compensation.

Section 21. Limitations of Special Privileges

The power of the State to act in the general welfare shall never be impaired by the making of any irrevocable grant of special privileges or immunities.

Section 22. Construction

The enumeration of rights and privileges shall not be construed to impair or deny others retained by the people.

Section 23. Marriage

The legislature shall have the power to reserve marriage to opposite-sex couples.

Section 24. Public Access to Information Concerning Persons Convicted of Certain Offenses Against Children and Certain Sexual Offenses

The public has a right of access to registration information regarding persons convicted of certain offenses against children and persons convicted of certain sexual offenses. The legislature shall determine which offenses are subject to this provision, what information constitutes registration information to which the public has a right of access, the manner of public access to the registration information and a period of time after which and conditions pursuant to which a convicted person may petition for termination of public access.

Section 25. Sexual Assault Crimes Against Minors

In continuous sexual assault crimes against minors younger than fourteen years of age, the legislature may define:

What behavior constitutes a continuing course of conduct; and
What constitutes the jury unanimity that is required for a conviction.

ARTICLE II: SUFFRAGE AND ELECTIONS

Section 1. Qualifications

Every citizen of the United States who shall have attained the age of eighteen years, have been a resident of this State not less than one year next preceding the election and be a voter registered as provided by law, shall be qualified to vote in any state or local election.

Section 2. Disqualification

No person who is non compos mentis shall be qualified to vote. No person convicted of a felony shall be qualified to vote except upon the person's final discharge or earlier as provided by law.

Section 3. Residence

No person shall be deemed to have gained or lost residence simply because of the person's presence or absence while employed in the service of the United States, or while engaged in navigation or while a student at any institution of learning.

Section 4. Registration; Voting

The legislature shall provide for the registration of voters and for absentee voting and shall prescribe the method of voting at all elections. Secrecy of voting shall be preserved; provided that no person shall be required to declare a party preference or nonpartisanship as a condition of voting in any primary or special primary election. Secrecy of voting and choice of political party affiliation or nonpartisanship shall be preserved.

Section 5. Campaign Fund, Spending Limit

The legislature shall establish a campaign fund to be used for partial public financing of campaigns for public offices of the State and its political subdivisions, as provided by law. The legislature shall provide a limit on the campaign spending of candidates.

Section 6. Campaign Contributions Limits

Limitations on campaign contributions to any political candidate, or authorized political campaign organization for such candidate, for any elective office within the State shall be provided by law.

Section 7. Resignation From Public Office

Any elected public officer shall resign from that office before being eligible as a candidate for another public office, if the term of the office sought begins before the end of the term of the office held.

Section 8. General, Special and Primary Elections

General elections shall be held on the first Tuesday after the first Monday in November in all even-numbered years. Special and primary elections may be held as provided by law; provided that in no case shall any primary election precede a general election by less than forty-five days.

Section 9. Presidential Preference Primary

A presidential preference primary may be held as provided by law.

Section 10. Contested Elections

Contested elections shall be determined by a court of competent jurisdiction in such manner as shall be provided by law.

ARTICLE III: THE LEGISLATURE

Section 1. Legislative Power

The legislative power of the State shall be vested in a legislature, which shall consist of two houses, a senate and a house of representatives. Such power shall extend to all rightful subjects of legislation not inconsistent with this constitution or the Constitution of the United States.

Section 2. Composition of Senate

The senate shall be composed of twenty-five members, who shall be elected by the qualified voters of the respective senatorial districts. Until the next reapportionment the senatorial districts and the number of senators to be elected from each shall be as set forth in the Schedule.

Section 3. Composition of House of Representatives

The house of representatives shall be composed of fifty-one members, who shall be elected by the qualified voters of the respective representative districts. Until the next reapportionment, the representative districts and the number of representatives to be elected from each shall be as set forth in the Schedule.

Section 4. Election of Members; Term

Each member of the legislature shall be elected at an election. If more than one candidate has been nominated for election to a seat in the legislature, the member occupying that seat shall be elected at a general election. If a candidate nominated for a seat at a primary election is unopposed for that seat at the general election, the candidate shall be deemed elected at the primary election. The term of office of a member of the house of representatives shall be two years and the term of office of a member of the senate shall be four years. The term of a member of the legislature shall begin on the day of the general election at which elected or if elected at a primary election, on the day of the general election immediately following the primary election at which elected. For a member of the house of representatives, the terms shall end on the day of the general election immediately following the day the member's term commences. For a member of the senate, the term shall end on the day of the second general election immediately following the day the member's term commences.

Section 5. Vacancies

Any vacancy in the legislature shall be filled for the unexpired term in such manner as may be provided by law, or, if no provision be made by law, by appointment by the governor for the unexpired term.

Section 6. Qualifications of Members

No person shall be eligible to serve as a member of the senate unless the person has been a resident of the State for not less than three years, has attained the age of majority and is, prior to filing nomination papers and thereafter continues to be, a qualified voter of the senatorial district from which the person seeks to be elected; except that in the year of the first general election following reapportionment, but prior to the primary election, an incumbent senator may move to a new district without being disqualified from completing the remainder of the incumbent senator's term. No person shall be eligible to serve as a member of the house of representatives unless the person has been a resident of the State for not less than three years, has attained the age of majority and is, prior to filing nomination papers and thereafter continues to be, a qualified voter of the representative district from which the person seeks to be elected; except that in the year of the first general election following reapportionment, but prior to the primary election, an incumbent representative may move to a new district without being disqualified from completing the remainder of the incumbent representative's term.

Section 7. Privileges of Members

No member of the legislature shall be held to answer before any other tribunal for any statement made or action taken in the exercise of the member's legislative functions; and members of the legislature shall, in all cases except felony or breach of the peace, be privileged from arrest during their attendance at the sessions of their respective houses, and in going to and returning from the same.

Section 8. Disqualifications of Members

No member of the legislature shall hold any other public office under the State, nor shall the member, during the term for which the member is elected or appointed, be elected or appointed to any public office or employment which shall have been created, or the emoluments whereof shall have been increased, by legislative act during such term. The term "public offices," for the purposes of this section, shall not include notaries public, reserve police officers or officers of emergency organizations for civilian defense or disaster relief. The legislature may prescribe further disqualifications.

Section 9. Legislative Allowance

The members of the legislature shall receive allowances reasonably related to expenses as provided by law.

Section 10. Sessions

The legislature shall convene annually in regular session at 10:00 o'clock a.m. on the third Wednesday in January.

At the written request of two-thirds of the members to which each house is entitled, the presiding officers of both houses shall convene the legislature in special session. At the written request of two-thirds of the members of the senate, the president of the senate shall convene the senate in special session for the purpose of carrying out its responsibility established by Section 3 of Article VI. The governor may convene both houses or the senate alone in special session.

Regular sessions shall be limited to a period of sixty days, and special sessions shall be limited to a period of thirty days. Any session may be extended a total of not more than fifteen days. Such extension shall be granted by the presiding officers of both houses at the written request of two-thirds of the members to which each house is entitled or may be granted by the governor. Each regular session shall be recessed for not less than five days at some period between the twentieth and fortieth days of the regular session. The legislature shall determine the dates of the mandatory recess by concurrent resolution. Any session may be recessed by concurrent resolution adopted by a majority of the members to which each house is entitled. Saturdays, Sundays, holidays, the days in mandatory recess and any days in recess pursuant to a concurrent resolution shall be excluded in computing the number of days of any session.

All sessions shall be held in the capital of the State. In case the capital shall be unsafe, the governor may direct that any session be held at some other place.

Section 11. Adjournment

Neither house shall adjourn during any session of the legislature for more than three days, or sine die, without the consent of the other.

Section 12. Organization; Discipline; Rules; Procedure

Each house shall be the judge of the elections, returns and qualifications of its own members and shall have, for misconduct, disorderly behavior or neglect of duty of any member, power to punish such member by censure or, upon a two-thirds vote of all the members to which such house is entitled, by suspension or expulsion of such member. Each house shall choose its own officers, determine the rules of its proceedings and keep a journal. The ayes and noes of the members on any question shall, at the desire of one-fifth of the members present, be entered upon the journal.

Twenty days after a bill has been referred to a committee in either house, the bill may be recalled from such committee by the affirmative vote of one-third of the members to which such house is entitled.

Every meeting of a committee in either house or of a committee comprised of a member or members from both houses held for the purpose of making decision on matters referred to the committee shall be open to the public.

By rule of its proceedings, applicable to both houses, each house shall provide for the date by which all bills to be considered in a regular session shall be introduced.

Section 13. Quorum; Compulsory Attendance

A majority of the number of members to which each house is entitled shall constitute a quorum of such house for the conduct of ordinary business, of which quorum a majority vote shall suffice; but the final passage of a bill in each house shall require the vote of a majority of all the members to which such house is entitled, taken by ayes and noes and entered upon its journal. A smaller number than a quorum may adjourn from day to day and may compel the attendance of absent members in such manner and under such penalties as each house may provide.

Section 14. Bills; Enactment

No law shall be passed except by bill. Each law shall embrace but one subject, which shall be expressed in its title. The enacting clause of each law shall be, "Be it enacted by the legislature of the State of Hawaii."

Section 15. Passage of Bills

No bill shall become law unless it shall pass three readings in each house on separate days. No bill shall pass third or final reading in either house unless printed copies of the bill in the form to be passed shall have been made available to the members of that house for at least forty-eight hours.
Every bill when passed by the house in which it originated, or in which amendments thereto shall have originated, shall immediately be certified by the presiding officer and clerk and sent to the other house for consideration.
Any bill pending at the final adjournment of a regular session in an odd-numbered year shall carry over with the same status to the next regular session. Before the carried-over bill is enacted, it shall pass at least one reading in the house in which the bill originated.

Section 16. Approval or Veto

Every bill which shall have passed the legislature shall be certified by the presiding officers and clerks of both houses and shall thereupon be presented to the governor. If the governor approves it, the governor shall sign it and it shall become law. If the governor does not approve such bill, the governor may return it, with the governor's objections to the legislature.
Except for items appropriated to be expended by the judicial and legislative branches, the governor may veto any specific item or items in any bill which appropriates money for specific purposes by striking out or reducing the same; but the governor shall veto other bills, if at all, only as a whole.

The governor shall have ten days to consider bills presented to the governor ten or more days before the adjournment of the legislature sine die, and if any such bill is neither signed nor returned by the governor within that time, it shall become law in like manner as if the governor had signed it.

Reconsideration After Adjournment

The governor shall have forty-five days, after the adjournment of the legislature sine die, to consider bills presented to the governor less than ten days before such adjournment, or presented after adjournment, and any such bill shall become law on the forty-fifth day unless the governor by proclamation shall have given ten days' notice to the legislature that the governor plans to return such bill with the governor's objections on that day. The legislature may convene at or before noon on the forty-fifth day in special session, without call, for the sole purpose of acting upon any such bill returned by the governor. In case the legislature shall fail to so convene, such bill shall not become law. Any such bill may be amended to meet the governor's objections and, if so amended and passed, only one reading being required in each house for such passage, it shall be presented again to the governor, but shall become law only if the governor shall sign it within ten days after presentation.

In computing the number of days designated in this section, the following days shall be excluded: Saturdays, Sundays, holidays and any days in which the legislature is in recess prior to its adjournment as provided in section 10 of this article.

Section 17. Procedures Upon Veto

Upon the receipt of a veto message from the governor, each house shall enter the same at large upon its journal and proceed to reconsider the vetoed bill, or the item or items vetoed, and again vote upon such bill, or such item or items, by ayes and noes, which shall be entered upon its journal. If after such reconsideration such bill, or such item or items, shall be approved by a two-thirds vote of all members to which each house is entitled, the same shall become law.

Section 18. Punishment of Nonmembers

Each house may punish by fine, or by imprisonment not exceeding thirty days, any person not a member of either house who shall be guilty of disrespect of such house by any disorderly or contemptuous behavior in its presence or that of any committee thereof; or who shall, on account of the exercise of any legislative function, threaten harm to the body or estate of any of the members of such house; or who shall assault, arrest or detain any witness or other person ordered to attend such house, on the witness' or other person's way going to or returning therefrom; or who shall rescue any person arrested by order of such house.

Any person charged with such an offense shall be informed in writing of the charge made against the person and have opportunity to present evidence and be heard in the person's own defense.

Section 19. Impeachment

The governor and lieutenant governor, and any appointive officer for whose removal the consent of the senate is required, may be removed from office upon conviction of impeachment for such causes as may be provided by law.

The house of representatives shall have the sole power of impeachment of the governor and lieutenant governor and the senate the sole power to try such impeachments, and no such officer shall be convicted without the concurrence of two-thirds of the members of the senate. When sitting for that purpose, the members of the senate shall be on oath or affirmation and the chief justice shall preside. Subject to the provisions of this paragraph, the legislature may provide for the manner and procedure of removal by impeachment of such officers.
The legislature shall by law provide for the manner and procedure of removal by impeachment of the appointive officers. Judgments in cases of impeachment shall not extend beyond

removal from office and disqualification to hold and enjoy any office of honor, trust or profit under the State; but the person convicted may nevertheless be liable and subject to indictment, trial, judgment and punishment as provided by law.

ARTICLE IV: REAPPORTIONMENT

Section 1. Reapportionment Years

The year 1973, the year 1981, and every tenth year thereafter shall be reapportionment years.

Section 2. Reapportionment Commission

A reapportionment commission shall be constituted on or before May 1 of each reapportionment year and whenever reapportionment is required by court order. The commission shall consist of nine members. The president of the senate and the speaker of the house of representatives shall each select two members. Members of each house belonging to the party or parties different from that of the president or the speaker shall designate one of their number for each house and the two so designated shall each select two members of the commission. The eight members so selected, promptly after selection, shall be certified by the selecting authorities to the chief election officer and within thirty days thereafter, shall select, by a vote of six members, and promptly certify to the chief election officer the ninth member who shall serve as chairperson of the commission. Each of the four officials designated above as selecting authorities for the eight members of the commission, at the time of the commission selections, shall also select one person from each basic island unit to serve on an apportionment advisory council for that island unit. The councils shall remain in existence during the life of the commission and each shall serve in an advisory capacity to the commission for matters affecting its island unit.

A vacancy in the commission or a council shall be filled by the initial selecting authority within fifteen days after the vacancy occurs. Commission and council positions and vacancies not filled within the times specified shall be filled promptly thereafter by the supreme court.

The commission shall act by majority vote of its membership and shall establish its own procedures, except as may be provided by law.

Not more than one hundred fifty days from the date on which its members are certified, the commission shall file with the chief election officer a reapportionment plan for the state legislature and a reapportionment plan for the United States congressional districts which shall become law after publication as provided by law. Members of the commission shall hold office until each reapportionment plan becomes effective or until such time as may be provided by law.

No member of the reapportionment commission or an apportionment advisory council shall be eligible to become a candidate for election to either house of the legislature or to the United States House of Representatives in either of the first two elections under any such reapportionment plan.

Commission and apportionment advisory council members shall be compensated and reimbursed for their necessary expenses as provided by law.

The chief election officer shall be secretary of the commission without vote and, under the direction of the commission, shall furnish all necessary technical services. The legislature shall appropriate funds to enable the commission to carry out its duties.

Section 3. Chief Election Officer

The legislature shall provide for a chief election officer of the State, whose responsibilities shall be as provided by law and shall include the supervision of state elections, the maximization of registration of eligible voters throughout the State and the maintenance of data concerning registered voters, elections, apportionment and districting.

Section 4. Apportionment Among Basic Island Units

The commission shall allocate the total number of members of each house of the state legislature being reapportioned among the four basic island units, namely:

(1) the island of Hawaii,

(2) the islands of Maui, Lanai, Molokai and Kahoolawe,

(3) the island of Oahu and all other islands not specifically enumerated, and

(4) the islands of Kauai and Niihau, using the total number of permanent residents in each of the basic island units and computed by the method known as the method of equal proportions; except that no basic island unit shall receive less than one member in each house.

Section 5. Minimum Representation for Basic Island Units

The representation of any basic island unit initially allocated less than a minimum of two senators and three representatives shall be augmented by allocating thereto the number of senators or representatives necessary to attain such minimums which number, notwithstanding the provisions of Sections 2 and 3 of Article III shall be added to the membership of the appropriate body until the next reapportionment. The senators or representatives of any basic island unit so augmented shall exercise a fractional vote wherein the numerator is the number initially allocated and the denominator is the minimum above specified.

Section 6. Apportionment Within Basic Island Units

Upon the determination of the total number of members of each house of the state legislature to which each basic island unit is entitled, the commission shall apportion the members among the districts therein and shall redraw district lines where necessary in such manner that for each house the average number of permanent residents per member in each district is as nearly equal to the average for the basic island unit as practicable.

In effecting such redistricting, the commission shall be guided by the following criteria:

1. No district shall extend beyond the boundaries of any basic island unit.

2. No district shall be so drawn as to unduly favor a person or political faction.

3. Except in the case of districts encompassing more than one island, districts shall be contiguous.

4. Insofar as practicable, districts shall be compact.

5. Where possible, district lines shall follow permanent and easily recognized features, such as streets, streams and clear geographical features, and, when practicable, shall coincide with census tract boundaries.

6. Where practicable, representative districts shall be wholly included within senatorial districts.

7. Not more than four members shall be elected from any district.

8. Where practicable, submergence of an area in a larger district wherein substantially different socio-economic interests predominate shall be avoided.

Section 7. Election of Senators After Reapportionment

Regardless of whether or not a senator is serving a term that would have extended past the general election at which an apportionment plan becomes effective, the term of office of all senators shall end at that general election. The staggered terms of senators in each district shall be recomputed as established by the next section in this article, and the number of senators in a senatorial district under the reapportionment plan of the commission.

Section 8. Staggered Terms for The Senate

The reapportionment commission shall, as part of the reapportionment plan, assign two-year terms for twelve senate seats for the election immediately following the adoption of the reapportionment plan. The remaining seats shall be assigned four-year terms. Insofar as practicable, the commission shall assign the two-year terms to senate seats so that the resident population of each senate district shall have no more than two regular senate elections for a particular senate seat within the six-year period beginning in the even-numbered year prior to the reapportionment year; provided that in the event of a multi-member senate district, the senators elected with the highest number of votes in that district in the election immediately following the adoption of the reapportionment plan shall fill the senate seats in that district which were assigned the four-year terms by the commission.

Section 9. Congressional Redistricting for United States House of Representatives

The commission shall, at such times as may be required by this article and as may be required by law of the United States, redraw congressional district lines for the districts from which the members of the United States House of Representatives allocated to this State by Congress are elected.

Section 10. Mandamus and Judicial Review

Original jurisdiction is vested in the supreme court of the State to be exercised on the petition of any registered voter whereby it may compel, by mandamus or otherwise, the appropriate person or persons to perform their duty or to correct any error made in a reapportionment plan, or it may take such other action to effectuate the purposes of this section as it may deem appropriate. Any such petition shall be filed within forty-five days of the date specified for any duty or within forty-five days after the filing of a reapportionment plan.

ARTICLE V: THE EXECUTIVE

Section 1. Establishment of The Executive

The executive power of the State shall be vested in a governor. The governor shall be elected by the qualified voters of this State at a general election. The person receiving the highest number of votes shall be the governor. In case of a tie vote, the selection of the governor shall be determined as provided by law.

The term of office of the governor shall begin at noon on the first Monday in December next following the governor's election and end at noon on the first Monday in December, four years thereafter.

No person shall be elected to the office of governor for more than two consecutive full terms.
No person shall be eligible for the office of governor unless the person shall be a qualified voter, have attained the age of thirty years and have been a resident of this State for five years immediately preceding the person's election.

The governor shall not hold any other office or employment of profit under the State or the United States during the governor's term of office.

Section 2. Lieutenant Governor

There shall be a lieutenant governor who shall have the same qualifications as the governor. The lieutenant governor shall be elected at the same time, for the same term and in the same manner as the governor; provided that the votes cast in the general election for the nominee for governor shall be deemed cast for the nominee for lieutenant governor of the same political party. No person shall be elected to the office of lieutenant governor for more than two consecutive full terms. The lieutenant governor shall perform such duties as may be provided by law.

Section 4. Succession to Governorship; Absence or Disability of Governor

When the office of governor is vacant, the lieutenant governor shall become governor. In the event of the absence of the governor from the State, or the governor's inability to exercise and discharge the powers and duties of the governor's office, such powers and duties shall devolve upon the lieutenant governor during such absence or disability.

When the office of lieutenant governor is vacant, or in the event of the absence of the lieutenant governor from the State, or the lieutenant governor's inability to exercise and discharge the powers and duties of the lieutenant governor's office, such powers and duties shall devolve upon such officers in such order of succession as may be provided by law.

In the event of the impeachment of the governor or of the lieutenant governor, the governor or the lieutenant governor shall not exercise the powers of the applicable office until acquitted.

Section 5. Executive Powers

The governor shall be responsible for the faithful execution of the laws. The governor shall be commander in chief of the armed forces of the State and may call out such forces to execute the laws, suppress or prevent insurrection or lawless violence or repel invasion. The governor shall, at the beginning of each session, and may, at other times, give to the legislature information concerning the affairs of the State and recommend to its consideration such measures as the governor shall deem expedient.

The governor may grant reprieves, commutations and pardons, after conviction, for all offenses, subject to regulation by law as to the manner of applying for the same. The legislature may, by general law, authorize the governor to grant pardons before conviction, to grant pardons for impeachment and to restore civil rights denied by reason of conviction of offenses by tribunals other than those of this State.

The governor shall appoint an administrative director to serve at the governor's pleasure.

Section 6. Executive and Administrative Offices and Departments

All executive and administrative offices, departments and instrumentalities of the state government and their respective powers and duties shall be allocated by law among and within not more than twenty principal departments in such a manner as to group the same according to common purposes and related functions. Temporary commissions or agencies for special purposes may be established by law and need not be allocated within a principal department.

Each principal department shall be under the supervision of the governor and, unless otherwise provided in this constitution or by law, shall be headed by a single executive. Such single executive shall be nominated and, by and with the advice and consent of the senate, appointed by the governor. That person shall hold office for a term to expire at the end of the term for which the governor was elected, unless sooner removed by the governor; except that the removal of the chief legal officer of the State shall be subject to the advice and consent of the senate.

Except as otherwise provided in this constitution, whenever a board, commission or other body shall be the head of a principal department of the state government, the members thereof shall be nominated and, by and with the advice and consent of the senate, appointed by the governor. The term of office and removal of such members shall be as provided by law. Such board, commission or other body may appoint a principal executive officer who, when authorized by law, may be an ex officio, voting member thereof, and who may be removed by a majority vote of the members appointed by the governor. The governor shall nominate and, by and with the advice and consent of the senate, appoint all officers for whose election or appointment provision is not otherwise provided for by this constitution or by law. If the manner or removal of an officer is not prescribed in this constitution, removal shall be as provided by law.

When the senate is not in session and a vacancy occurs in any office, appointment to which requires the confirmation of the senate, the governor may fill the office by granting a commission which shall expire, unless such appointment is confirmed, at the end of the next session of the senate. The person so appointed shall not be eligible for another interim appointment to such office if the appointment failed to be confirmed by the senate. No person who has been nominated for appointment to any office and whose appointment has not received the consent of the senate shall be eligible to an interim appointment thereafter to such office.

Every officer appointed under the provisions of this section shall be a citizen of the United States and shall have been a resident of this State for at least one year immediately preceding that person's appointment, except that this residency requirement shall not apply to the president of the University of Hawaii.

ARTICLE VI: THE JUDICIARY

Section 1. Judicial Power

The judicial power of the State shall be vested in one supreme court, one intermediate appellate court, circuit courts, district courts and in such other courts as the legislature may from time to time establish. The several courts shall have original and appellate jurisdiction as provided by law and shall establish time limits for disposition of cases in accordance with their rules.

Section 2. Supreme Court; Intermediate Appellate Court; Circuit Courts

The supreme court shall consist of a chief justice and four associate justices. The chief justice may assign a judge or judges of the intermediate appellate court or a circuit court to serve temporarily on the supreme court, a judge of the circuit court to serve temporarily on the intermediate appellate court and a judge of the district court to serve temporarily on the circuit court. As provided by law, at the request of the chief justice, retired justices of the supreme court also may serve temporarily on the supreme court, and retired judges of the intermediate appellate court, the circuit courts, the district courts and the district family courts may serve temporarily on the intermediate appellate court, on any circuit court, on any district court and on any district family court, respectively. In case of a vacancy in the office of chief justice, or if the chief justice is ill, absent or otherwise unable to serve, an associate justice designated in accordance with the rules of the supreme court shall serve temporarily in place of the chief justice.

Section 3. Appointment of Justices And Judges

The governor, with the consent of the senate, shall fill a vacancy in the office of the chief justice, supreme court, intermediate appellate court and circuit courts, by appointing a person from a list of not less than four, and not more than six, nominees for the vacancy, presented to the governor by the judicial selection commission.

If the governor fails to make any appointment within thirty days of presentation, or within ten days of the senate's rejection of any previous appointment, the appointment shall be made by the judicial selection commission from the list with the consent of the senate. If the senate fails to reject any appointment within thirty days thereof, it shall be deemed to have given its consent to such appointment. If the senate shall reject any appointment, the governor shall make another appointment from the list within ten days thereof. The same appointment and consent procedure shall be followed until a valid appointment has been made, or failing this, the commission shall make the appointment from the list, without senate consent.

The chief justice, with the consent of the senate, shall fill a vacancy in the district courts by appointing a person from a list of not less than six nominees for the vacancy presented by the judicial selection commission. If the chief justice fails to make the appointment within thirty days of presentation, or within ten days of the senate's rejection of any previous appointment, the appointment shall be made by the judicial selection commission from the list with the consent of the senate. The senate shall hold a public hearing and vote on each appointment within thirty days of any appointment. If the senate fails to do so, the nomination shall be returned to the commission and the commission shall make the appointment from the list without senate consent. The chief justice shall appoint per diem district court judges as provided by law.

The judicial selection commission shall disclose to the public the list of nominees for each vacancy concurrently with the presentation of each list to the governor or the chief justice, as applicable.

Qualifications for Appointment

Justices and judges shall be residents and citizens of the State and of the United States, and licensed to practice law by the supreme court. A justice of the supreme court, a judge of the intermediate appellate court and a judge of the circuit court shall have been so licensed for a period of not less than ten years preceding nomination. A judge of the district court shall have been so licensed for a period of not less than five years preceding nomination.

No justice or judge shall, during the term of office, engage in the practice of law, or run for or hold any other office or position of profit under the United States, the State or its political subdivisions.

Tenure; Retirement

The term of office of justices and judges of the supreme court, intermediate appellate court and circuit courts shall be ten years. Judges of district courts shall hold office for the periods as provided by law. At least six months prior to the expiration of a justice's or judge's term of office, every justice and judge shall petition the judicial selection commission to be retained in office or shall inform the commission of an intention to retire. If the judicial selection commission determines that the justice or judge should be retained in office, the commission shall renew the term of office of the justice or judge for the period provided by this section or by law.

Justices and judges shall be retired upon attaining the age of seventy years. They shall be included in any retirement law of the State.

Section 4. Judicial Selection Commission

There shall be a judicial selection commission that shall consist of nine members. The governor shall appoint two members to the commission. No more than one of the two members shall be a licensed attorney. The president of the senate and the speaker of the house of representatives shall each respectively appoint two members to the commission. The chief justice of the supreme court shall appoint one member to the commission. Members in good standing of the bar of the State shall elect two of their number to the commission in an election conducted by the supreme court or its delegate. No more than four members of the commission shall be licensed attorneys. At all times, at least one member of the commission shall be a resident of a county other than the City and County of Honolulu.

The commission shall be selected and shall operate in a wholly nonpartisan manner. After the initial formation of the commission, elections and appointments to the commission shall be for staggered terms of six years each. Notwithstanding the foregoing, no member of the commission shall serve for more than six years on the commission.

Each member of the judicial selection commission shall be a resident of the State and a citizen of the United States. No member shall run for or hold any other elected office under the United States, the State or its political subdivisions. No member shall take an active part in political management or in political campaigns. No member shall be eligible for appointment to the judicial office of the State so long as the person is a member of the judicial commission and for a period of three years thereafter. No act of the judicial selection commission shall be valid except by concurrence of the majority of its voting members.
The judicial selection commission shall select one of its members to serve as chairperson. The commission shall adopt rules which shall have the force and effect of law. The deliberations of the commission shall be confidential.

The legislature shall provide for the staff and operating expenses of the judicial selection commission in a separate budget. No member of the judicial selection commission shall receive any compensation for commission services, but shall be allowed necessary expenses for travel, board and lodging incurred in the performance of commission duties.

The judicial selection commission shall be attached to the judiciary branch of the state government for purposes of administration.

Section 5. Retirement; Removal; Discipline

The supreme court shall have the power to reprimand, discipline, suspend with or without salary, retire or remove from office any justice or judge for misconduct or disability, as provided by rules adopted by the supreme court.
The supreme court shall create a commission on judicial discipline which shall have authority to investigate and conduct hearings concerning allegations of misconduct or disability and to make recommendations to the supreme court concerning reprimand, discipline, suspension, retirement or removal of any justice or judge.

Section 6. Administration

The chief justice of the supreme court shall be the administrative head of the courts. The chief justice may assign judges from one circuit court to another for temporary service. With the approval of the supreme court, the chief justice shall appoint an administrative director to serve at the chief justice's pleasure.

Section 7. Rules

The supreme court shall have power to promulgate rules and regulations in all civil and criminal cases for all courts relating to process, practice, procedure and appeals, which shall have the force and effect of law.

ARTICLE VII: TAXATION AND FINANCE

Section 1. Taxing Power Inalienable

The power of taxation shall never be surrendered, suspended or contracted away.

Section 2. Income Taxation

In enacting any law imposing a tax on or measured by income, the legislature may define income by reference to provisions of the laws of the United States as they may be or become effective at any time or from time to time, whether retrospective or prospective in their operation. The legislature may provide that amendments to such laws of the United States shall become the law of the State upon their becoming the law of the United States. The legislature shall in any such law set the rate or rates of such tax. The legislature may in so defining income make exceptions, additions or modifications to any provisions of the laws of the United States so referred to and provide for retrospective exceptions or modifications to those provisions which are retrospective.

Section 3. Tax Review Commission

There shall be a tax review commission, which shall be appointed as provided by law on or before July 1, 1980, and every five years thereafter. The commission shall submit to the legislature an evaluation of the State's tax structure, recommend revenue and tax policy and then dissolve.

Section 4. Appropriations for Private Purposes Prohibited

No tax shall be levied or appropriation of public money or property made, nor shall the public credit be used, directly or indirectly, except for a public purpose. No grant shall be made in violation of Section 4 of Article I of this constitution. No grant of public money or property shall be made except pursuant to standards provided by law.

Section 5. Expenditure Controls

Provision for the control of the rate of expenditures of appropriated state moneys, and for the reduction of such expenditures under prescribed conditions, shall be made by law. No public money shall be expended except pursuant to appropriations made by law. General fund expenditures for any fiscal year shall not exceed the State's current general fund revenues and unencumbered cash balances, except when the governor publicly declares the public health, safety or welfare is threatened as provided by law.

Section 6. Disposition of Excess Revenues

Whenever the state general fund balance at the close of each of two successive fiscal years exceeds five percent of general fund revenues for each of the two fiscal years, the legislature in the next regular session shall:

Provide for a tax refund or tax credit to the taxpayers of the State, as provided by law;

Make a deposit into one or more funds, as provided by law, which shall serve as temporary supplemental sources of funding for the State in times of an emergency, economic downturn, or unforeseen reduction in revenue, as provided by law; or Appropriate general funds for the pre-payment of either or both of the following, as provided by law:

(A) Debt service for general obligation bonds issued by the State; or

(B) Pension or other post-employment benefit liabilities accrued for state employees.

For the purpose of this paragraph, "pre-payment" means a payment for a fiscal year in excess of the minimum payment required for that fiscal year by bond covenant or law.

Section 7. Council on Revenues

There shall be established by law a council on revenues which shall prepare revenue estimates of the state government and shall report the estimates to the governor and the legislature at times provided by law. The estimates shall be considered by the governor in preparing the budget, recommending appropriations and revenues and controlling expenditures. The estimates shall be considered by the legislature in appropriating funds and enacting revenue measures. All revenue estimates submitted by the council to the governor and the legislature shall be made public. If the legislature in appropriating funds or if the governor in preparing the budget or recommending appropriations exceeds estimated revenues due to proposed expenditures, this fact shall be made public including the reasons therefor.

Section 8. The Budget

Within such time prior to the opening of each regular session in an odd-numbered year as may be provided by law, the governor shall submit to the legislature a budget in a form provided by law setting forth a complete plan of proposed expenditures of the executive branch, estimates as provided by law of the aggregate expenditures of the judicial and legislative branches, and anticipated receipts of the State for the ensuing fiscal biennium, together with such other information as the legislature may require. A complete plan of proposed expenditures of the judicial branch for the ensuing fiscal biennium shall be submitted by the chief justice to the legislature in a form and within such time prior to the opening of each regular session in an odd-numbered year as shall be provided by law. The budget prepared by the governor and the plan of proposed expenditures prepared by the chief justice shall also be submitted in bill form. The governor shall also, upon the opening of each such session, submit bills to provide for such proposed expenditures and for any recommended additional revenues or borrowings by which the proposed expenditures are to be met. The proposed general fund expenditures in the plan of proposed expenditures, including estimates of the aggregate expenditures of the judicial and legislative branches, submitted by the governor shall not exceed the general fund expenditure ceiling established by the legislature under section 9 of this article; provided that proposed general fund expenditures in the plan may exceed such ceiling if the governor sets forth the dollar amount and the rate by which the ceiling will be exceeded and the reasons therefor.

Section 9. Legislative Appropriations; Procedures; Expenditure Ceiling

In each regular session in an odd-numbered year, the legislature shall transmit to the governor an appropriation bill or bills providing for the anticipated total expenditures of the State for the ensuing fiscal biennium. In such session, no appropriation bill, except bills recommended by the governor for immediate passage, or to cover the expenses of the legislature, shall be passed on final reading until the bill authorizing operating expenditures for the ensuing fiscal biennium, to be known as the general appropriations bill, shall have been transmitted to the governor.

In each regular session in an even-numbered year, at such time as may be provided by law, the governor may submit to the legislature a bill to amend any appropriation for operating expenditures of the current fiscal biennium, to be known as the supplemental appropriations bill, and bills to amend any appropriations for capital expenditures of the current fiscal biennium, and at the same time the governor shall submit a bill or bills to provide for any added revenues or borrowings that such amendments may require. In each regular session in an even-numbered year, bills may be introduced in the legislature to amend any appropriation act or bond authorization act of the current fiscal biennium or prior fiscal periods. In any such session in which the legislature submits to the governor a supplemental appropriations bill, no other appropriation bill, except bills recommended by the governor for immediate passage, or to cover the expenses of the legislature, shall be passed on final reading until such supplemental appropriations bill shall have been transmitted to the governor.

General Fund Expenditure Ceiling

Notwithstanding any other provision to the contrary, the legislature shall establish a general fund expenditure ceiling which shall limit the rate of growth of general fund appropriations, excluding federal funds received by the general fund, to the estimated rate of growth of the State's economy as provided by law. No appropriations in excess of such ceiling shall be authorized during any legislative session unless the legislature shall, by a two-thirds vote of the members to which each house of the legislature is entitled, set forth the dollar amount and the rate by which the ceiling will be exceeded and the reasons therefor.

Section 10. Auditor

The legislature, by a majority vote of each house in joint session, shall appoint an auditor who shall serve for a period of eight years and thereafter until a successor shall have been appointed. The legislature, by a two-thirds vote of the members in joint session, may remove the auditor from office at any time for cause. It shall be the duty of the auditor to conduct post-audits of the transactions, accounts, programs and performance of all departments, offices and agencies of the State and its political subdivisions, to certify to the accuracy of all financial statements issued by the respective accounting officers and to report the auditor's findings and recommendations to the governor and to the legislature at such times as shall be provided by law. The auditor shall also make such additional reports and conduct such other investigations as may be directed by the legislature.

Section 11. Lapsing of Appropriations

All appropriations for which the source is general obligation bond funds or general funds shall be for specified periods. No such appropriation shall be made for a period exceeding three years; provided that appropriations from the state educational facilities improvement special fund may be made for periods exceeding three years to allow for construction or acquisition of public school facilities. Any such appropriation or any portion of any such appropriation that is unencumbered at the close of the fiscal period for which the appropriation is made shall lapse; provided that no appropriation for which the source is general obligation bond funds nor any portion of any such appropriation shall lapse if the legislature determines that the appropriation or any portion of the appropriation is necessary to qualify for federal aid financing and reimbursement. Where general obligation bonds have been authorized for an appropriation, the amount of the bond authorization shall be reduced in an amount equal to the amount lapsed.

Section 12. Definitions; Issuance of Indebtedness

For the purposes of this article:

1. The term "bonds" shall include bonds, notes and other instruments of indebtedness.

2. The term "general obligation bonds" means all bonds for the payment of the principal and interest of which the full faith and credit of the State or a political subdivision are pledged and, unless otherwise indicated, includes reimbursable general obligation bonds.

3. The term "net revenues" or "net user tax receipts" means the revenues or receipts derived from:
a. A public undertaking, improvement or system remaining after the costs of operation, maintenance and repair of the public undertaking, improvement or system, and the required payments

of the principal of and interest on all revenue bonds issued therefor, have been made; or

b. Any payments or return on security under a loan program or a loan thereunder, after the costs of operation and administration of the loan program, and the required payments of the principal of and interest on all revenue bonds issued therefor, have been made.

4. The term "dam and reservoir owner" means any person who has a right to, title to, or an interest in, a dam, a reservoir, or the property upon which a dam, a reservoir, or appurtenant work is located or proposed to be located.

5. The term "person" means an individual, firm, partnership, corporation, association, cooperative or other legal entity, governmental body or agency, board, bureau or other instrumentality thereof, or any combination of the foregoing.

6. The term "rates, rentals and charges" means all revenues and other moneys derived from the operation or lease of a public undertaking, improvement or system, or derived from any payments or return on security under a loan program or a loan thereunder; provided that insurance premium payments, assessments and surcharges, shall constitute rates, rentals and charges of a state property insurance program.

7. The term "reimbursable general obligation bonds" means general obligation bonds issued for a public undertaking, improvement or system from which revenues, or user taxes, or a combination of both, may be derived for the payment of the principal and interest as reimbursement to the general fund and for which reimbursement is required by law, and, in the case of general obligation bonds issued by the State for a political subdivision, general obligation bonds for which the payment of the principal and interest as reimbursement to the general fund is required by law to be made from the revenue of the political subdivision.

8. The term "revenue bonds" means all bonds payable from the revenues, or user taxes, or any combination of both, of a public undertaking, improvement, system or loan program and any loan made thereunder and secured as may be provided by law, including a loan program to provide loans to a state property insurance program providing hurricane insurance coverage to the general public.

9. The term "special purpose revenue bonds" means all bonds payable from rental or other payments made to an issuer by a person pursuant to contract and secured as may be provided by law.

10. The term "user tax" means a tax on goods or services or on the consumption thereof, the receipts of which are substantially derived from the consumption, use or sale of goods and services in the utilization of the functions or services furnished by a public undertaking, improvement or system; provided that mortgage recording taxes shall constitute user taxes of a state property insurance program.

The legislature, by a majority vote of the members to which each house is entitled, shall authorize the issuance of all general obligation bonds, bonds issued under special improvement statutes and revenue bonds issued by or on behalf of the State and shall prescribe by general law the manner and procedure for such issuance. The legislature by general law shall authorize political subdivisions to issue general obligation bonds, bonds issued under special improvement statutes and revenue bonds and shall prescribe the manner and procedure for such issuance. All such bonds issued by or on behalf of a political subdivision shall be authorized by the governing body of such political subdivision.

Special purpose revenue bonds shall only be authorized or issued to finance facilities of or for, or to loan the proceeds of such bonds to assist:

1. Manufacturing, processing or industrial enterprises;

2. Utilities serving the general public;

3. Health care facilities provided to the general public by not-for-profit corporations;

4. Early childhood education and care facilities provided to the general public by not-for-profit corporations;

5. Low and moderate income government housing programs;

6. Not-for-profit private nonsectarian and sectarian elementary schools, secondary schools, colleges and universities;

7. Agricultural enterprises; or

8. Dam and reservoir owners; provided that the bonds are issued for and the proceeds are used to offer loans to assist dam and reservoir owners to improve their facilities to protect public safety and provide significant benefits to the general public as important water sources, each of which is hereinafter referred to in this paragraph as a special purpose entity.

The legislature, by a two-thirds vote of the members to which each house is entitled, may enact enabling legislation for the issuance of special purpose revenue bonds separately for each special purpose entity, and, by a two-thirds vote of the members to which each house is entitled and by separate legislative bill, may authorize the State to issue special purpose revenue bonds for each single project or multi-project program of each special purpose entity; provided that the issuance of such special purpose revenue bonds is found to be in the public interest by the legislature; and provided further that the State may combine into a single issue of special purpose revenue bonds two or more proposed issues of special purpose revenue bonds to assist:

(1) Not-for-profit private nonsectarian and sectarian elementary schools, secondary schools, colleges, and universities;

(2) Dam and reservoir owners; or

(3) Agricultural enterprises, separately authorized as aforesaid, in the total amount not exceeding the aggregate of the proposed separate issues of special purpose revenue bonds. The legislature may enact enabling legislation to authorize political subdivisions to issue special purpose revenue bonds. If so authorized, a political subdivision by a two-thirds vote of the members to which its governing body is entitled and by separate ordinance may authorize the issuance of special purpose revenue bonds for each single project or multi-project program of each special purpose entity; provided that the issuance of such special purpose revenue bonds is found to be in the public interest by the governing body of the political subdivision. No special purpose revenue bonds shall be secured directly or indirectly by the general credit of the issuer or by any revenues or taxes of the issuer other than receipts derived from payments by a person or persons under contract or from any security for such contract or contracts or special purpose revenue bonds and no moneys other than such receipts shall be applied to the payment thereof. The governor shall provide the legislature in November of each year with a report on the cumulative amount of all special purpose revenue bonds authorized and issued, and such other information as may be necessary.

Section 13. Debt Limit; Exclusions

General obligation bonds may be issued by the State; provided that such bonds at the time of issuance would not cause the total amount of principal and interest payable in the current or any future fiscal year, whichever is higher, on such bonds and on all outstanding general obligation bonds to exceed: a sum equal to twenty percent of the average of the general fund revenues of the State in the three fiscal years immediately preceding such issuance until June 30, 1982; and thereafter, a sum equal to eighteen and one-half percent of the average of the general fund revenues of the State in the three fiscal years immediately preceding such issuance. Effective July 1, 1980, the legislature shall include a declaration of findings in every general law authorizing the issuance of general obligation bonds that the total amount of principal and interest, estimated for such bonds and for all bonds authorized and unissued and calculated for all bonds issued and outstanding, will not cause the debt limit to be exceeded at the time of issuance. Any bond issue by or on behalf of the State may exceed the debt limit if an emergency condition is declared to exist by the governor and concurred to by a two-thirds vote of the members to which each house of the legislature is entitled. For the purpose of this paragraph, general fund revenues of the State shall not include moneys received as grants from the federal government and receipts in reimbursement of any reimbursable general obligation bonds which are excluded as permitted by this section.

A sum equal to fifteen percent of the total of the assessed values for tax rate purposes of real property in each political subdivision, as determined by the last tax assessment rolls pursuant to law, is established as the limit of the funded debt of such political subdivision that is outstanding and unpaid at any time.
All general obligation bonds for a term exceeding two years shall be in serial form maturing in substantially equal installments of principal, or maturing in substantially equal installments of both principal and interest. The first installment of principal of general obligation bonds and of reimbursable general obligation bonds shall mature not later than five years from the date of issue of such series. The last installment on general obligation bonds shall mature not later than twenty-five years from the date of such issue and the last installment on general obligation bonds sold to the federal government, on reimbursable general obligation bonds and on bonds constituting instruments of indebtedness under which the State or a political subdivision incurs a contingent liability as a guarantor shall mature not later than thirty-five years from the date of such issue. The interest and principal payments of general obligation bonds shall be a

first charge on the general fund of the State or political subdivision, as the case may be.

In determining the power of the State to issue general obligation bonds or the funded debt of any political subdivision under section 12, the following shall be excluded:

1. Bonds that have matured, or that mature in the then current fiscal year, or that have been irrevocably called for redemption and the redemption date has occurred or will occur in the then fiscal year, or for the full payment of which moneys or securities have been irrevocably set aside.

2. Revenue bonds, if the issuer thereof is obligated by law to impose rates, rentals and charges for the use and services of the public undertaking, improvement or system or the benefits of a loan program or a loan thereunder or to impose a user tax, or to impose a combination of rates, rentals and charges and user tax, as the case may be, sufficient to pay the cost of operation, maintenance and repair, if any, of the public undertaking, improvement or system or the cost of maintaining a loan program or a loan thereunder and the required payments of the principal of and interest on all revenue bonds issued for the public undertaking, improvement or system or loan program, and if the issuer is obligated to deposit such revenues or tax or a combination of both into a special fund and to apply the same to such payments in the amount necessary therefor.

3. Special purpose revenue bonds, if the issuer thereof is required by law to contract with a person obligating such person to make rental or other payments to the issuer in an amount at least sufficient to make the required payment of the principal of and interest on such special purpose revenue bonds.

4. Bonds issued under special improvement statutes when the only security for such bonds is the properties benefited or improved or the assessments thereon.

5. General obligation bonds issued for assessable improvements, but only to the extent that reimbursements to the general fund for the principal and interest on such bonds are in fact made from assessment collections available therefor.

6. Reimbursable general obligation bonds issued for a public undertaking, improvement or system but only to the extent that reimbursements to the general fund are in fact made from the net revenue, or net user tax receipts, or combination of both, as determined for the immediately preceding fiscal year.

7. Reimbursable general obligation bonds issued by the State for any political subdivision, whether issued before or after the effective date of this section, but only for as long as reimbursement by the political subdivision to the State for the payment of principal and interest on such bonds is required by law; provided that in the case of bonds issued after the effective date of this section, the consent of the governing body of the political subdivision has first been obtained; and provided further that during the period that such bonds are excluded by the State, the principal amount then outstanding shall be included within the funded debt of such political subdivision.

8. Bonds constituting instruments of indebtedness under which the State or any political subdivision incurs a contingent liability as a guarantor, but only to the extent the principal amount of such bonds does not exceed seven percent of the principal amount of outstanding general obligation bonds not otherwise excluded under this section; provided that the State or political subdivision shall establish and maintain a reserve in an amount in reasonable proportion to the outstanding loans guaranteed by the State or political subdivision as provided by law.

9. Bonds issued by or on behalf of the State or by any political subdivision to meet appropriations for any fiscal period in anticipation of the collection of revenues for such period or to meet casual deficits or failures of revenue, if required to be paid within one year, and bonds issued by or on behalf of the State to suppress insurrection, to repel invasion, to defend the State in war or to meet emergencies caused by disaster or act of God. The total outstanding indebtedness of the State or funded debt of any political subdivision and the exclusions therefrom permitted by this section shall be made annually and certified by law or as provided by law. For the purposes of section 12 and this section, amounts received from on-street parking may be considered and treated as revenues of a parking undertaking. Nothing in section 12 or in this section shall prevent the refunding of any bond at any time.

ARTICLE VIII: LOCAL GOVERNMENT

Section 1. Creation; Powers of Political Subdivisions

The legislature shall create counties, and may create other political subdivisions within the State, and provide for the government thereof. Each political subdivision shall have and exercise such powers as shall be conferred under general laws.

Section 2. Local Self-Government; Charter

Each political subdivision shall have the power to frame and adopt a charter for its own self-government within such limits and under such procedures as may be provided by general law. Such procedures, however, shall not require the approval of a charter by a legislative body.

Charter provisions with respect to a political subdivision's executive, legislative and administrative structure and organization shall be superior to statutory provisions, subject to the authority of the legislature to enact general laws allocating and reallocating powers and functions.

A law may qualify as a general law even though it is inapplicable to one or more counties by reason of the provisions of this section.

Section 3. Taxation and Finance

The taxing power shall be reserved to the State, except so much thereof as may be delegated by the legislature to the political subdivisions, and except that all functions, powers and duties relating to the taxation of real property shall be exercised exclusively by the counties, with the exception of the county of Kalawao. The legislature shall have the power to apportion state revenues among the several political subdivisions.

Section 4. Mandates; Accrued Claims

No law shall be passed mandating any political subdivision to pay any previously accrued claim.

Section 5. Transfer Of Mandated Programs

If any new program or increase in the level of service under an existing program shall be mandated to any of the political subdivisions by the legislature, it shall provide that the State share in the cost.

Section 6. Statewide Laws

This article shall not limit the power of the legislature to enact laws of statewide concern.

ARTICLE IX: PUBLIC HEALTH AND WELFARE

Section 1. Public Health

The State shall provide for the protection and promotion of the public health.

Section 2. Care of Handicapped Persons

The State shall have the power to provide for the treatment and rehabilitation of handicapped persons.

Section 3. Public Assistance

The State shall have the power to provide financial assistance, medical assistance and social services for persons who are found to be in need of and are eligible for such assistance and services as provided by law.

Section 4. Economic Security of The Elderly

The State shall have the power to provide for the security of the elderly by establishing and promoting programs to assure their economic and social well-being.

Section 5. Housing, Slum Clearance, Development and Rehabilitation

The State shall have the power to provide for, or assist in, housing, slum clearance and the development or rehabilitation of substandard areas. The exercise of such power is deemed to be for a public use and purpose.

Section 6. Management Of State Population Growth

The State and its political subdivisions, as provided by general law, shall plan and manage the growth of the population to protect and preserve the public health and welfare; except that each political subdivision, as provided by general law, may plan and manage the growth of its population in a more restrictive manner than the State.

Section 7. Public Sightliness and Good Order

The State shall have the power to conserve and develop objects and places of historic or cultural interest and provide for public sightliness and physical good order. For these purposes private property shall be subject to reasonable regulation.

Section 8. Preservation of a Healthful Environment

The State shall have the power to promote and maintain a healthful environment, including the prevention of any excessive demands upon the environment and the State's resources.

Section 9. Cultural Resources

The State shall have the power to preserve and develop the cultural, creative and traditional arts of its various ethnic groups.

Section 10. Public Safety

The law of the splintered paddle, mamala-hoe kanawai, decreed by Kamehameha I--Let every elderly person, woman and child lie by the roadside in safety--shall be a unique and living symbol of the State's concern for public safety.

The State shall have the power to provide for the safety of the people from crimes against persons and property.

ARTICLE X: EDUCATION

Section 1. Public Education

The State shall provide for the establishment, support and control of a statewide system of public schools free from sectarian control, a state university, public libraries and such other educational institutions as may be deemed desirable, including physical facilities therefor. There shall be no discrimination in public educational institutions because of race, religion, sex or ancestry; nor shall public funds be appropriated for the support or benefit of any sectarian or nonsectarian private educational institution, except that proceeds of special purpose revenue bonds authorized or issued under section 12 of Article VII may be appropriated to finance or assist:

1. Not-for-profit corporations that provide early childhood education and care facilities serving the general public; and

2. Not-for-profit private nonsectarian and sectarian elementary schools, secondary schools, colleges and universities.

Section 2. Board of Education

There shall be a board of education. The governor shall nominate and, by and with the advice and consent of the senate, appoint the members of the board of education, as provided by law.

Section 3. Power of The Board of Education

The board of education shall have the power, as provided by law, to formulate statewide educational policy and appoint the superintendent of education as the chief executive officer of the public school system.

Section 4. Hawaiian Education Program

The State shall promote the study of Hawaiian culture, history and language.

The State shall provide for a Hawaiian education program consisting of language, culture and history in the public schools. The use of community expertise shall be encouraged as a suitable and essential means in furtherance of the Hawaiian education program.

Section 5. University of Hawaii

The University of Hawaii is hereby established as the state university and constituted a body corporate. It shall have title to all the real and personal property now or hereafter set aside or conveyed to it, which shall be held in public trust for its purposes, to be administered and disposed of as provided by law.

Section 6. Board of Regents; Powers

There shall be a board of regents of the University of Hawaii, the members of which shall be nominated and, by and with the advice and consent of the senate, appointed by the governor from pools of qualified candidates presented to the governor by the candidate advisory council for the board of regents of the University of Hawaii, as provided by law. At least part of the membership of the board shall represent geographic subdivisions of the State. The board shall have the power to formulate policy, and to exercise control over the university through its executive officer, the president of the university, who shall be appointed by the board. The board shall also have exclusive jurisdiction over the internal structure, management, and operation of the university. This section shall not limit the power of the legislature to enact laws of statewide concern. The legislature shall have the exclusive jurisdiction to identify laws of statewide concern.

ARTICLE XI: CONSERVATION, CONTROL AND DEVELOPMENT OF RESOURCES

Section 1. Conservation and Development of Resources

For the benefit of present and future generations, the State and its political subdivisions shall conserve and protect Hawaii's natural beauty and all natural resources, including land, water, air, minerals and energy sources, and shall promote the development and utilization of these resources in a manner consistent with their conservation and in furtherance of the self-sufficiency of the State.

All public natural resources are held in trust by the State for the benefit of the people.

Section 2. Management and Disposition of Natural Resources

The legislature shall vest in one or more executive boards or commissions powers for the management of natural resources owned or controlled by the State, and such powers of disposition thereof as may be provided by law; but land set aside for public use, other than for a reserve for conservation purposes, need not be placed under the jurisdiction of such a board or commission.

The mandatory provisions of this section shall not apply to the natural resources owned by or under the control of a political subdivision or a department or agency thereof.

Section 3. Agricultural Lands

The State shall conserve and protect agricultural lands, promote diversified agriculture, increase agricultural self-sufficiency and assure the availability of agriculturally suitable lands. The legislature shall provide standards and criteria to accomplish the foregoing.

Lands identified by the State as important agricultural lands needed to fulfill the purposes above shall not be reclassified by the State or rezoned by its political subdivisions without meeting the standards and criteria established by the legislature and approved by a two-thirds vote of the body responsible for the reclassification or rezoning action.

Section 4. Public Land Banking

The State shall have the power to acquire interests in real property to control future growth, development and land use within the State. The exercise of such power is deemed to be for a public use and purpose.

Section 5. General Laws Required; Exceptions

The legislative power over the lands owned by or under the control of the State and its political subdivisions shall be exercised only by general laws, except in respect to transfers to or for the use of the State, or a political subdivision, or any department or agency thereof.

Section 6. Marine Resources

The State shall have the power to manage and control the marine, seabed and other resources located within the boundaries of the State, including the archipelagic waters of the State, and reserves to itself all such rights outside state boundaries not specifically limited by federal or international law. All fisheries in the sea waters of the State not included in any fish pond, artificial enclosure or state-licensed mariculture operation shall be free to the public, subject to vested rights and the right of the State to regulate the same; provided that mariculture operations shall be established under guidelines enacted by the legislature, which shall protect the public's use and enjoyment of the reefs. The State may condemn such vested rights for public use.

Section 7. Water Resources

The State has an obligation to protect, control and regulate the use of Hawaii's water resources for the benefit of its people.

The legislature shall provide for a water resources agency which, as provided by law, shall set overall water conservation, quality and use policies; define beneficial and reasonable uses; protect ground and surface water resources, watersheds and natural stream environments; establish criteria for water use priorities while assuring appurtenant rights and existing correlative and riparian uses and establish procedures for regulating all uses of Hawaii's water resources.

Section 8. Nuclear Energy

No nuclear fission power plant shall be constructed or radioactive material disposed of in the State without the prior approval by a two-thirds vote in each house of the legislature.

Section 9. Environmental Rights

Each person has the right to a clean and healthful environment, as defined by laws relating to environmental quality, including control of pollution and conservation, protection and enhancement of natural resources. Any person may enforce this right against any party, public or private, through appropriate legal proceedings, subject to reasonable limitations and regulation as provided by law.

Section 10. Farm and Home Ownership

The public lands shall be used for the development of farm and home ownership on as widespread a basis as possible, in accordance with procedures and limitations prescribed by law.

Section 11. Exclusive Economic Zone

The State of Hawaii asserts and reserves its rights and interest in its exclusive economic zone for the purpose of exploring, exploiting, conserving and managing natural resources, both living and nonliving, of the seabed and subsoil, and superadjacent waters..

ARTICLE XII: HAWAIIAN AFFAIRS

Section 1. Hawaiian Homes Commission Act

Anything in this constitution to the contrary notwithstanding, the Hawaiian Homes Commission Act, 1920, enacted by the Congress, as the same has been or may be amended prior to the admission of the State, is hereby adopted as a law of the State, subject to amendment or repeal by the legislature; provided that if and to the extent that the United States shall so require, such law shall be subject to amendment or repeal only with the consent of the United States and in no other manner; provided further that if the United States shall have been provided or shall provide that particular provisions or types of provisions of such Act may be amended in the manner required for ordinary state legislation, such provisions or types of provisions may be so amended. The proceeds and income from Hawaiian home lands shall be used only in accordance with the terms and spirit of such Act. The legislature shall make sufficient sums available for the following purposes: (1) development of home, agriculture, farm and ranch lots; (2) home, agriculture, aquaculture, farm and ranch loans; (3) rehabilitation projects to include, but not limited to, educational, economic, political, social and cultural processes by which the general welfare and conditions of native Hawaiians are thereby improved; (4) the administration and operating budget of the department of Hawaiian home lands; in furtherance of (1), (2), (3) and (4) herein, by appropriating the same in the manner provided by law.

Thirty percent of the state receipts derived from the leasing of cultivated sugarcane lands under any provision of law or from water licenses shall be transferred to the native Hawaiian rehabilitation fund, section 213 of the Hawaiian Homes Commission Act, 1920, for the purposes enumerated in that section. Thirty percent of the state receipts derived from the leasing of lands cultivated as sugarcane lands on the effective date of this section shall continue to be so transferred to the native Hawaiian rehabilitation fund whenever such lands are sold, developed, leased, utilized, transferred, set aside or otherwise disposed of for purposes other than the cultivation of sugarcane. There shall be no ceiling established for the aggregate amount transferred into the native Hawaiian rehabilitation fund.

Section 2. Acceptance of Compact

The State and its people do hereby accept, as a compact with the United States, or as conditions or trust provisions imposed by the United States, relating to the management and disposition of the Hawaiian home lands, the requirement that section 1 hereof be included in this constitution, in whole or in part, it being intended that the Act or acts of the Congress pertaining thereto shall be definitive of the extent and nature of such compact, conditions or trust provisions, as the case may be. The State and its people do further agree and declare that the spirit of the Hawaiian Homes Commission Act looking to the continuance of the Hawaiian homes projects for the further rehabilitation of the Hawaiian race shall be faithfully carried out.

Section 3. Compact Adoption; Procedures After Adoption

As a compact with the United States relating to the management and disposition of the Hawaiian home lands, the Hawaiian Homes Commission Act, 1920, as amended, shall be adopted as a provision of the constitution of this State, as provided in section 7, subsection (b), of the Admission Act, subject to amendment or repeal only with the consent of the United States, and in no other manner; provided that (1) sections 202, 213, 219, 220, 222, 224 and 225 and other provisions relating to administration, and paragraph (2) of section 204, sections 206 and 212 and other provisions relating to the powers and duties of officers other than those charged with the administration of such Act, may be amended in the constitution, or in the manner required for state legislation, but the Hawaiian home-loan fund, the Hawaiian home-operating fund and the Hawaiian home-development fund shall not be reduced or impaired by any such amendment, whether made in the constitution or in the manner required for state legislation, and the encumbrances authorized to be placed on Hawaiian home lands by officers other than those charged with the administration of such Act, shall not be increased, except with the consent of the United States; (2) that any amendment to increase the benefits to lessees of Hawaiian home lands may be made in the constitution, or in the manner required for state legislation, but the qualifications of lessees shall not be changed except with the consent of the United States; and (3) that all proceeds and income from the "available lands," as defined by such Act, shall be used only in carrying out the provisions of such Act.

Section 4. Public Trust

The lands granted to the State of Hawaii by Section 5(b) of the Admission Act and pursuant to Article XVI, Section 7, of the State Constitution, excluding therefrom lands defined as "available lands" by Section 203 of the Hawaiian Homes Commission Act, 1920, as amended, shall be held by the State as a public trust for native Hawaiians and the general public.

Section 5. Office of Hawaiian Affairs; Establishment of Board of Trustees

There is hereby established an Office of Hawaiian Affairs. The Office of Hawaiian Affairs shall hold title to all the real and personal property now or hereafter set aside or conveyed to it which shall be held in trust for native Hawaiians and Hawaiians. There shall be a board of trustees for the Office of Hawaiian Affairs elected by qualified voters who are Hawaiians, as provided by law. The board members shall be Hawaiians. There shall be not less than nine members of the board of trustees; provided that each of the following Islands have one representative: Oahu, Kauai, Maui, Molokai and Hawaii. The board shall select a chairperson from its members.

Section 6. Powers of Board of Trustees

The board of trustees of the Office of Hawaiian Affairs shall exercise power as provided by law: to manage and administer the proceeds from the sale or other disposition of the lands, natural resources, minerals and income derived from whatever sources for native Hawaiians and Hawaiians, including all income and proceeds from that pro rata portion of the trust referred to in section 4 of this article for native Hawaiians; to formulate policy relating to affairs of native Hawaiians and Hawaiians; and to exercise control over real and personal property set aside by state, federal or private sources and transferred to the board for native Hawaiians and Hawaiians. The board shall have the power to exercise control over the Office of Hawaiian Affairs through its executive officer, the administrator of the Office of Hawaiian Affairs, who shall be appointed by the board.

Section 7. Traditional and Customary Rights

The State reaffirms and shall protect all rights, customarily and traditionally exercised for subsistence, cultural and religious purposes and possessed by ahupua'a tenants who are descendants of native Hawaiians who inhabited the Hawaiian Islands prior to 1778, subject to the right of the State to regulate such rights.

ARTICLE XIII: ORGANIZATION; COLLECTIVE BARGAINING

Section 1. Private Employees

Persons in private employment shall have the right to organize for the purpose of collective bargaining.

Section 2. Public Employees

Persons in public employment shall have the right to organize for the purpose of collective bargaining as provided by law.

ARTICLE XIV: CODE OF ETHICS

The people of Hawaii believe that public officers and employees must exhibit the highest standards of ethical conduct and that these standards come from the personal integrity of each individual in government. To keep faith with this belief, the legislature, each political subdivision and the constitutional convention shall adopt a code of ethics which shall apply to appointed and elected officers and employees of the State or the political subdivision, respectively, including members of the boards, commissions and other bodies.

Each code of ethics shall be administered by a separate ethics commission, except the code of ethics adopted by the constitutional convention which shall be administered by the state ethics commission. The members of ethics commissions shall be prohibited from taking an active part in political management or in political campaigns. Ethics commissioners shall be selected in a manner which assures their independence and impartiality.

Each code of ethics shall include, but not be limited to, provisions on gifts, confidential information, use of position, contracts with government agencies, post-employment, financial disclosure and lobbyist registration and restriction. The financial disclosure provisions shall require all elected officers, all candidates for elective office and such appointed officers and employees as provided by law to make public financial disclosures. Other public officials having significant discretionary or fiscal powers as provided by law shall make confidential financial disclosures. All financial disclosure statements shall include, but not be limited to, sources and amounts of income, business ownership, officer and director positions, ownership of real property, debts, creditor interests in insolvent businesses and the names of persons represented before government agencies.

ARTICLE XV: STATE BOUNDARIES; CAPITAL; FLAG; LANGUAGE AND MOTTO

Section 1. Boundaries

The State of Hawaii shall consist of all the islands, together with their appurtenant reefs and territorial and archipelagic waters, included in the Territory of Hawaii on the date of enactment of the Admission Act, except the atoll known as Palmyra Island, together with its appurtenant reefs and territorial waters; but this State shall not be deemed to include the Midway Islands, Johnston Island, Sand Island (offshore from Johnston Island) or Kingman Reef, together with their appurtenant reefs and territorial waters.

Section 2. Capital

Honolulu, on the island of Oahu, shall be the capital of the State.

Section 3. State Flag

The Hawaiian flag shall be the flag of the State.

Section 4. Official Languages

English and Hawaiian shall be the official languages of Hawaii, except that Hawaiian shall be required for public acts and transactions only as provided by law.

Section 5. Motto

The motto of the State shall be, "Ua mau ke ea o ka aina i ka pono."

ARTICLE XVI: GENERAL AND MISCELLANEOUS PROVISIONS

Section 1. Civil Service

The employment of persons in the civil service, as defined by law, of or under the State, shall be governed by the merit principle.

Section 2. Employee Retirement System

Membership in any employees' retirement system of the State or any political subdivision thereof shall be a contractual relationship, the accrued benefits of which shall not be diminished or impaired.

Section 3. Disqualifications From Public Office or Employment; Salary Commission

No person shall hold any public office or employment who has been convicted of any act to overthrow, or attempt to overthrow, or conspiracy with any person to overthrow the government of this State or of the United States by force or violence.

Section [3.5]. There shall be a commission on salaries as provided by law, which shall review and recommend salaries for the justices and judges of all state courts, members of the legislature, department heads or executive officers of the executive departments and the deputies or assistants to department heads of the executive departments as provided by law, excluding the University of Hawaii and the department of education. The commission shall also review and make recommendations for the salary of the administrative director of the State or equivalent position and the salary of the governor and the lieutenant governor.

Any salary established pursuant to this section shall not be decreased during a term of office, unless by general law applying to all salaried officers of the State.

Not later than the fortieth legislative day of the 2007 regular legislative session and every six years thereafter, the commission shall submit to the legislature its recommendations and then dissolve.

The recommended salaries submitted shall become effective as provided in the recommendation, unless the legislature disapproves the entire recommendation as a whole by adoption of a concurrent resolution prior to adjournment sine die of the legislative session in which the recommendation is submitted; provided that any change in salary which becomes effective shall not apply to the legislature to which the recommendation for the change in salary was submitted.

Section 4. Oath of Office

All eligible public officers, before entering upon the duties of their respective offices, shall take and subscribe to the following oath or affirmation: "I do solemnly swear (or affirm) that I will support and defend the Constitution of the United States, and the Constitution of the State of Hawaii, and that I will faithfully discharge my duties as .... to best of my ability." As used in this section, "eligible public officers" means the governor, the lieutenant governor, the members of both houses of the legislature, the members of the board of education, the members of the national guard, State or county employees who possess police powers, district court judges, and all those whose appointment requires the consent of the senate.

Section 5. Intergovernmental Relations

The legislature may provide for cooperation on the part of this State and its political subdivisions with the United States, or other states and territories, or their political subdivisions, in matters affecting the public health, safety and general welfare. Funds may be appropriated to effect such cooperation.

Section 6. Federal Lands

The United States shall be vested with or retain title to or an interest in or shall hold the property in the Territory of Hawaii set aside for the use of the United States and remaining so set aside immediately prior to the admission of this State, in all respects as and to the extent set forth in the act or resolution providing for the admission of this State to the Union.

Section 7. Compliance with Trust

Any trust provisions which the Congress shall impose, upon the admission of this State, in respect of the lands patented to the State by the United States or the proceeds and income therefrom, shall be complied with by appropriate legislation. Such legislation shall not diminish or limit the benefits of native Hawaiians under Section 4 of Article XII.

Section 8. Administration of Undisposed Lands

All provisions of the Act of Congress approved March 18, 1959 reserving rights or powers to the United States, as well as those prescribing the terms or conditions of the grants of lands or other property therein made to the State of Hawaii are consented to fully by the State and its people.

Section 9. Tax Exemption of Federal Property

No taxes shall be imposed by the State upon any lands or other property now owned or hereafter acquired by the United States, except as the same shall become taxable by reason of disposition thereof by the United States or by reason of the consent of the United States to such taxation.

Section 10. Hawaii National Park

All provisions of the act or resolution admitting this State to the Union, or providing for such admission, which reserve to the United States jurisdiction of Hawaii National Park, or the ownership or control of lands within Hawaii National Park, are consented to fully by the State and its people.

Section 11. Judicial Rights

All those provisions of the act or resolution admitting this State to the Union, or providing for such admission, which reserve to the United States judicial rights or powers are consented to fully by the State and its people; and those provisions of such act or resolution which preserve judicial rights and powers for the State are hereby accepted and adopted, and such rights and powers are hereby assumed, to be exercised and discharged pursuant to this constitution and the laws of the State.

Section 12. Quieting Title

No person shall be deprived of title to an estate or interest in real property by another person claiming actual, continuous, hostile, exclusive, open and notorious possession of such lands, except to real property of five acres or less. Such claim may be asserted in good faith by any person not more than once in twenty years.

Section 13. Plain Language

Insofar as practicable, all governmental writing meant for the public, in whatever language, should be plainly worded, avoiding the use of technical terms.

Section 14. Titles, Subtitles; Construction

Titles and subtitles shall not be used for purposes of construing this constitution.

Section 15. General Power

The enumeration in this constitution of specified powers shall not be construed as limitations upon the power of the State to provide for the general welfare of the people.

Section 16. Provisions are Self-Executing

The provisions of this constitution shall be self-executing to the fullest extent that their respective natures permit.

ARTICLE XVII: REVISION AND AMENDMENT

Section 1. Methods of Proposal

Revisions of or amendments to this constitution may be proposed by constitutional convention or by the legislature.

Section 2. Constitutional Convention

The legislature may submit to the electorate at any general or special election the question, "Shall there be a convention to propose a revision of or amendments to the Constitution?" If any nine-year period shall elapse during which the question shall not have been submitted, the lieutenant governor shall certify the question, to be voted on at the first general election following the expiration of such period.

Election of Delegates

If a majority of the ballots cast upon such a question be in the affirmative, delegates to the convention shall be chosen at the next regular election unless the legislature shall provide for the election of delegates at a special election.
Notwithstanding any provision in this constitution to the contrary, other than Section 3 of Article XVI, any qualified voter of the district concerned shall be eligible to membership in the convention.

The legislature shall provide for the number of delegates to the convention, the areas from which they shall be elected and the manner in which the convention shall convene. The legislature shall also provide for the necessary facilities and equipment for the convention. The convention shall have the same powers and privileges, as nearly as practicable, as provided for the convention of 1978.

Meeting

The constitutional convention shall convene not less than five months prior to the next regularly scheduled general election.

Organization; Procedure

The convention shall determine its own organization and rules of procedure. It shall be the sole judge of the elections, returns and qualifications of its members and, by a two-thirds vote, may suspend or remove any member for cause. The governor shall fill any vacancy by appointment of a qualified voter from the district concerned.

Ratification; Appropriations

The convention shall provide for the time and manner in which the proposed constitutional revision or amendments shall be submitted to a vote of the electorate; provided that each amendment shall be submitted in the form of a question embracing but one subject; and provided further, that each question shall have designated spaces to mark YES or NO on the amendment.

At least thirty days prior to the submission of any proposed revision or amendments, the convention shall make available for public inspection, a full text of the proposed amendments. Every public library, office of the clerk of each county, and the chief election officer shall be provided such texts and shall make them available for public inspection. The full text of any proposed revision or amendments shall also be made available for inspection at every polling place on the day of the election at which such revision or amendments are submitted.

The convention shall, as provided by law, be responsible for a program of voter education concerning each proposed revision or amendment to be submitted to the electorate.
The revision or amendments shall be effective only if approved at

a general election by a majority of all the votes tallied upon the question, this majority constituting at least fifty per cent of the total vote cast at the election, or at a special election by a majority of all the votes tallied upon the question, this majority constituting at least thirty per cent of the total number of registered voters.

The provisions of this section shall be self-executing, but the legislature shall make the necessary appropriations and may enact legislation to facilitate their operation.

Section 3. Amendments Proposed By Legislature

The legislature may propose amendments to the constitution by adopting the same, in the manner required for legislation, by a two-thirds vote of each house on final reading at any session, after either or both houses shall have given the governor at least ten days written notice of the final form of the proposed amendment, or, with or without such notice, by a majority vote of each house on final reading at each of two successive sessions.

Upon such adoption, the proposed amendments shall be entered upon the journals, with the ayes and noes, and published once in each of four successive weeks in at least one newspaper of general circulation in each senatorial district wherein such a newspaper is published, within the two months period immediately preceding the next general election.

At such general election the proposed amendments shall be submitted to the electorate for approval or rejection upon a separate ballot.

The conditions of and requirements for ratification of such proposed amendments shall be the same as provided in section 2 of this article for ratification at a general election.

Section 4. Veto

No proposal for amendment of the constitution adopted in either manner provided by this article shall be subject to veto by the governor.

Section 5. Conflicting Revisions or Amendments

If a revision or amendment proposed by a constitutional convention is in conflict with a revision or amendment proposed by the legislature and both are submitted to the electorate at the same election and both are approved, then the revision or amendment proposed by the convention shall prevail. If conflicting revisions or amendments are proposed by the same body and are submitted to the electorate at the same election and both are approved, then the revision or amendment receiving the highest number of votes shall prevail.

ARTICLE XVIII: SCHEDULE

Section 1. Districting and Apportionment

Omitted.

Section 2. 1978 Senatorial Elections

Article III, Section 4, to the contrary notwithstanding, the terms of office of the members of the senate elected in the 1978 general election shall be as follows: members of the senate shall be divided into two classes. The first class shall consist of the following number elected with the highest number of votes from their respective senatorial districts: first district, one; second district, one; third district, one; fourth district, two; fifth district, two; sixth district, two; seventh district, two; eighth district, one. Members of the first class shall hold office for a term of four years beginning with their election and ending on the day of the second general election held thereafter. The remaining members elected shall constitute the second class and shall hold office for a term of two years beginning with their election and ending on the day of the next general election held thereafter.

Section 3. Salaries of Legislators

Repealed.

Section 4. Effective Date for Term Limitations for Governor and Lieutenant Governor

The amendments to Sections 1 and 2 of Article V shall limit the term of any person elected to the office of governor or lieutenant governor in the 1978 general election to two consecutive full terms commencing from noon on the first Monday in December, 1978.

Section 5. Judiciary: Transition; Effective Date

The three members initially appointed to the judicial selection commission by the governor shall serve for terms of two, four and six years respectively. The members initially appointed to the commission by the president of the senate and the speaker of the house of representatives shall serve for two years. The two members initially appointed to the commission by the chief justice of the supreme court shall serve terms of four and six years respectively. The two members initially elected to the commission by the members of the bar of the State shall serve for terms of four and six years respectively. The current terms of justices and judges in office shall terminate as heretofore provided by law, subject to earlier termination and removal as provided in Article VI. The amendments to Article VI shall take effect upon ratification. The judicial selection commission shall be created no later than April 1, 1979.

Section 6. Effective Date and Application of Real Property Tax Transfer

The amendment to Section 3 of Article VIII shall take effect on the first day of July after two full calendar years have elapsed following the ratification of such amendment [November 7, 1978]; provided that for a period of eleven years following such ratification, the policies and methods of assessing real property taxes shall be uniform throughout the State and shall be established by agreement of a majority of the political subdivisions. Each political subdivision shall enact such uniform policies and methods of assessment by ordinance before the effective date of this amendment [July 1, 1981], and in the event the political subdivisions fail to enact such ordinances, the uniform policies and methods of assessment shall be established by general law. Any amendments to the uniform policies and methods of assessment established by the political subdivisions may only be made by agreement of a majority of the political subdivisions and enactment thereof by ordinance in each political subdivision.

Real property tax exemptions and dedications of land for specific use for assessment at its value in such use as provided by law and in effect upon ratification of the amendment to Section 3 of Article VIII [November 7, 1978] shall be enacted by ordinance and shall not be eliminated or diminished for a period of eleven years following such ratification; provided that increases in such exemptions, or the additions of new and further exemptions or dedications of lands, may be established or granted only by agreement of a majority of the political subdivisions, and such increases or additions shall be enacted by ordinance in each political subdivision.

Section 7. 1978 Board of Education Elections

Members elected to the board of education in the 1978 general election shall serve for two-year terms.

Section 8. Effective Date for Office of Hawaiian Affairs

The legislature shall provide for the implementation of the amendments to Article XII in Sections 5 and 6 on or before the first general election following ratification of the amendments to Article XII in Sections 5 and 6.

Section 9. Continuity of Laws

All laws in force at the time amendments to this constitution take effect that are not inconsistent with the constitution as amended shall remain in force, mutatis mutandis, until they expire by their own limitations or are amended or repealed by the legislature.

Except as otherwise provided by amendments to this constitution, all existing writs, actions, suits, proceedings, civil or criminal liabilities, prosecutions, judgments, sentences, orders, decrees, appeals, causes of action, contracts, claims, demands, titles and rights shall continue unaffected notwithstanding the taking effect of the amendments and may be maintained, enforced or prosecuted, as the case may be, before the appropriate or corresponding tribunals or agencies of or under the State or of the United States, in all respects as fully as could have been done prior to the taking effect of the amendments.

Section 10. Debts

The debts and liabilities of the Territory shall be assumed and paid by the State, and all debts owed to the Territory shall be collected by the State.

Section 11. Residence, Other Qualifications

Requirements as to residence, citizenship or other status or qualifications in or under the State prescribed by this constitution shall be satisfied pro tanto by corresponding residence, citizenship or other status or qualifications in or under the Territory.

Section 12. Board of Education Transition

There shall be a period of transition from the elected to the appointed board of education, as provided by law.

Effective Date

This constitution shall take effect and be in full force immediately upon the admission of Hawaii into the Union as a State. Done in Convention, at Iolani Palace, Honolulu, Hawaii, on the twenty-second day of July, in the year one thousand nine hundred fifty and of the Independence of the United States of America the one hundred and seventy-fifth.

www.ingramcontent.com/pod-product-compliance
Lightning Source LLC
Chambersburg PA
CBHW051532240526
45471CB00019B/751